WATFORD

C000145853

THIS BOO
BELONGS

Name:	Age:

Favourite player:

2018/2019

My Predictions...   Actual...

The Hornets' final position:

The Hornets' top scorer:

Premier League Winners:*

Premier League top scorer:

FA Cup Winners:

EFL Cup Winners:

Contributors: Peter Rogers & Steve Scott

A TWOCAN PUBLICATION

©2018. Published by twocan under licence from Watford FC.

Every effort has been made to ensure the accuracy of information within this publication but the publishers cannot be held responsible for any errors or omissions. Views expressed are those of the authors and do not necessarily represent those of the publishers or the football club. All rights reserved.

ISBN 978-1-912692-31-6

£8.99

PICTURE CREDITS: Alan Cozzi, Action Images and Press Association.

CONTENTS

WATFORD

Squad 2018/19	**6**
Practice Makes Perfect	16
Daryl Janmaat Poster	**18**
Stat Attack: Luther Blissett	19
Danger Men	**20**
Magic Moment: We're Going to Wembley	24
Étienne Capoue Poster	**25**
Fantastic	26
#Boy'sGotSkills: The Puskas Move	**28**
Colour Roberto Pereyra	29
Troy Deeney Poster	**30**
Stat Attack: John Barnes	31
Player of the Season	**32**
Goal of the Season	33
Guess the Club	**34**
Local Heroes	36
Magic Moment: Going Up	**38**

Will Hughes Poster	**39**
Who are Yer?	**40**
Isaac Success Poster	42
#Boy'sGotSkills: The Flip Flap	**43**
Rewind	44
2017/18 End of Term Exam	**45**
Fast Forward	46
2018/19 Predictions	**47**
#Boy'sGotSkills: The Okocha Step Over	48
Ben Foster Poster	**49**
Great Gaffers	50
First Eleven	**52**
Spot the Ball / What Ball?	53
Abdoulaye Doucouré Poster	**54**
Stat Attack: Ashley Young	55
Hero Hunt	**56**
Shirt Shuffle	57
Magic Moment: Play-Off Drama	**58**
Andre Gray Poster	59
Hey Ref!	**60**
Answers	62

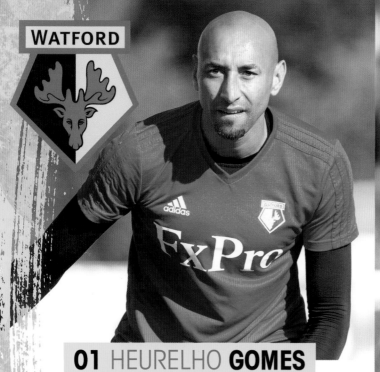

01 HEURELHO **GOMES**

GOALKEEPER   BORN: 15/02/1981 · BRAZIL

A towering shot-stopper, Gomes joined the Hornets from Tottenham back in July 2014 and quickly became the club's number one. He played a crucial role in the club's promotion to the Premier League and earned the Player of the Season trophy in 2015/16.

02 DARYL **JANMAAT**

DEFENDER   BORN: 22/07/1989 · NETHERLANDS

Janmaat signed for Watford in August 2016 from Newcastle United. He battled with Femenía for the right-back spot in 2017/18 but capped the season with a fine run and finish against Chelsea at The Vic that won him the Goal of the Season award.

SQUAD 2018/19

03 MIGUEL **BRITOS**

DEFENDER   BORN: 17/07/1985 · URUGUAY

An imposing defender, Britos scored a dramatic late equaliser in a thrilling 3-3 draw against Liverpool on the opening day of the 2017/18 campaign, but injury restricted him to just twelve appearances last season.

04 YOUNÈS **KABOUL**

DEFENDER **BORN: 04/01/1986 · FRANCE**

A talented centre-half, Kaboul joined Watford in August 2016. He is a former captain of the France Under-21 team and has played five times for the full national side.

05 SEBASTIAN **PRÖDL**

DEFENDER **BORN: 21/06/1987 · AUSTRIA**

An Austrian international, Prödl added a wealth of experience to the Hornets' back-line when he joined in July 2015, having previously played in the Champions League and Europa League during his time at Werder Bremen.

06 ADRIAN **MARIAPPA**

DEFENDER **BORN: 03/10/1986 · JAMAICA**

Mariappa made a surprise but welcome return to Watford in 2016. As ever, he put in solid performances during the 2017/18 season - and even captained the side against Tottenham Hotspur at Wembley.

WATFORD

07 GERARD **DEULOFEU**

MIDFIELDER **BORN: 13/04/1994 · SPAIN**

After a spell on loan last season, Deulofeu made the move permanent and signed a five-year deal with the Hornets. An exciting winger who can play off either flank, he has Premier League experience from two spells with Everton.

08 TOM **CLEVERLEY**

MIDFIELDER **BORN: 12/08/1989 · ENGLAND**

After two separate loan spells, the Hornets got their man on a permanent basis in March 2017. A tireless midfielder, Cleverley had a moment to remember as he lashed home a late winner against Arsenal during an impressive 2017/18 campaign.

09 TROY **DEENEY**

FORWARD **BORN: 29/06/1988 · ENGLAND**

Deeney joined Watford in 2010 and is a firm favourite. Last season he found the net on five occasions, including goals against Chelsea, Man United and Arsenal, and two important strikes against Everton and West Brom that virtually ensured the Hornets' safety in the Premier League.

11 ADAM **MASINA**

DEFENDER · BORN: 02/01/1994 · ITALY

A 6ft 3in full-back, Masina completed a permanent transfer from Bologna to Watford in early July 2018. Morocco-born Masina is a former Italy Under-21 international who made 131 appearances for Bologna, including 99 in Serie A.

10 ISAAC **SUCCESS**

FORWARD · BORN: 07/01/1996 · NIGERIA

Success agreed a five-year contract at Vicarage Road in July 2016, completing a club transfer record breaking move. He scored his first Watford goal in a 2-2 draw at home to AFC Bournemouth that season.

12 KEN **SEMA**

MIDFIELDER · BORN: 30/09/1993 · SWEDEN

Sema joined the Golden Boys from Swedish over-achievers Östersunds in July 2018. The fleet-footed winger signed a five-year deal with the Hornets, having impressed during his time in his home country.

15 CRAIG **CATHCART**

DEFENDER BORN: 06/02/1989 · NORTHERN IRELAND

Cathcart signed with the Hornets back in June 2014. He battled back from a knee injury to play seven times in the Premier League in 2017/18, playing five consecutive full games at the end of the campaign.

14 NATHANIEL **CHALOBAH**

MIDFIELDER BORN: 12/12/1994 · ENGLAND

Chalobah signed a five-year deal at Vicarage Road in July 2017. He played 97 times for England at various youth levels, and was a key part of the Under-21s' run to the semi-final of the European Championships in 2017.

16 ABDOULAYE **DOUCOURÉ**

MIDFIELDER BORN: 01/01/1993 · FRANCE

An outstanding 2017/18 campaign - in which Doucouré scored seven goals - saw him pick up both the Player of the Season and Players' Player of the Season trophies, and he committed his long-term future to the club by signing a new five-year contract at the start of August 2018.

19 WILL **HUGHES**

MIDFIELDER   BORN: 17/04/1995 · ENGLAND

A creative midfielder, Hughes joined the Hornets from Championship side Derby County in July 2017. He has an racked up and impressive amount of experience, with nearly 190 Rams appearances before joining the Hornets in the top flight.

18 ANDRE **GRAY**

FORWARD   BORN: 26/06/1991 · ENGLAND

Watford secured the signing of Gray from Burnley in August 2017 for a club record fee. A pacy centre-forward, he made 31 Premier League appearances - scoring five goals in his debut season for the Hornets.

WATFORD

20 DOMINGOS **QUINA**

MIDFIELDER · **BORN: 18/11/1999** · **PORTUGAL**

Quina joined Watford in a deadline day move from West Ham in August 2018. A bright young prospect, he played a starring role as Portugal were crowned champions in the 2018 Under-19 European Championships.

21 KIKO **FEMENÍA**

DEFENDER · **BORN: 02/02/1991** · **SPAIN**

Femenía joined the Hornets in July 2017. He showed his talent, making 23 appearances in his debut season and netted his first Watford goal by opening the scoring in a 2-2 draw against Bournemouth in March 2018.

22 MARVIN **ZEEGELAAR**

DEFENDER · **BORN: 12/08/1990** · **NETHERLANDS**

Zeegelaar joined the Hornets from Sporting Lisbon in August 2017. Although he struggled to cement himself as a first team regular during his debut season, he showed flashes of brilliance. His two assists against Newcastle in a 3-0 win showed the quality the Dutchman can possess.

23 MARC **NAVARRO**

DEFENDER   BORN: 02/07/1995 · SPAIN

Navarro progressed through the youth system at Barcelona and joined Watford from Espanyol this summer. He made his La Liga debut in January 2017 with Espanyol, scoring in a 3-1 win over Granada and went on to make 36 appearances, scoring three times in the Spanish top flight.

24 BEN **WILMOT**

DEFENDER   BORN: 04/11/1999 · ENGLAND

The Hornets fought off competition from some of the country's biggest clubs for the England Under-19 international in the summer of 2018. He made 15 appearances for Stevenage last season, earning him the League 2 Apprentice of the Year award.

25 JOSÉ **HOLEBAS**

DEFENDER   BORN: 27/06/1984 · GREECE

A left-sided operator, Holebas has a wealth of top-level domestic experience and European pedigree as well, with 23 Champions League appearances to his name across his time in Italy and Greece. In 2017/18, he claimed four assists over the course of the Premier League season in 28 appearances for the Hornets.

26 BEN **FOSTER**

GOALKEEPER   BORN: 03/04/1983 · ENGLAND

Watford legend Ben Foster rejoined the club in July 2018. He won the club's Player of the Season award for the 2006/07 season, even though Watford were relegated; the glove-man's performances in goal won him many admirers.

29 ÉTIENNE **CAPOUE**

MIDFIELDER   BORN: 11/07/1988 · FRANCE

Capoue made 26 appearances in all competitions in 2017/18 - scoring in every competition the Hornets took part in, with goals against Bristol City in the EFL Cup and FA Cup, as well as a strike against Bournemouth in the Premier League.

27 CHRISTIAN **KABASELE**

DEFENDER   BORN: 24/02/1991 · BELGIUM

Kabasele developed a reputation as a goalscorer during his first season with the Hornets in 2016/17, chipping in with three goals in just 18 appearances. He went on to make 28 appearances in 2017/18 and found the back of the net against Everton and Tottenham Hotspur.

30 PONTUS **DAHLBERG**

GOALKEEPER BORN: 21/01/1999 · SWEDEN

A promising Sweden Under-21 goalkeeper, Dahlberg signed with the Hornets in January 2018 from IFK Göteborg. The 6ft 4in stopper played 47 times for IFK in total, including once in the Europa League, attracting much interest thanks to a string of fine performances in goal.

33 STEFANO **OKAKA**

FORWARD BORN: 09/08/1989 · ITALY

Okaka hit the ground running in 2017/18 as he scored in the Hornets' opening game of the season at home to Liverpool, however he was limited to just 16 appearances - mostly from the bench - in a frustrating campaign.

37 ROBERTO **PEREYRA**

MIDFIELDER BORN: 07/01/1991 · ARGENTINA

A tenacious midfielder, Pereyra made 32 Premier League appearances last season and scored five goals as well as playing important roles in wins against Chelsea and Newcastle.

PRACTICE MAKES PERFECT...

Practice, preparation and perseverance are all well-known key ingredients to success in the modern game. Long before the Hornets run out at Vicarage Road, they will have gone through a thorough and detailed spell of work at the club's busy training centre.

The Hornets' training ground is geared up to ensure that Javi Gracia's men are fully equipped for the Premier League challenges that lie ahead. The modern-day player will not only be given the best of surfaces to practice on, but also given the very best advice and guidance in terms of their fitness, diet, rest and mental approach to performing at their maximum.

A typical day will begin with a series of physical tests, being weighed and taking part in a number of aerobic exercises, before blood levels and heart rates are measured.

Diet is vital to any player's wellbeing and performance levels, so a suitable breakfast is provided before the players head to the gymnasium to enjoy their own personal work-outs.

Prior to taking to the training pitches, players will be provided with a GPS tracking system and heart rate analysis monitors ensuring that all they do can be measured, monitored and reviewed. Then the physical conditioning begins out on the pitches. The manager and coaches will get down to working on various drills, set-piece situations and practice matches in the day's main session.

After a warm-down programme, it's off for a healthy lunch and a return to the gym for a strength, power and injury presentation session and feedback on the day's activities will be provided to the manager, coaches and players by the sports science department.

Come match day, this is where all the team's hard work and dedication through the week will make the difference.

DARYL
JANMAAT

BORN:

1 FEBRUARY 1958 · FALMOUTH, JAMAICA

POSITION:

STRIKER

HORNETS DEBUT:

WATFORD 1-0 BARNSLEY
DIVISION FOUR · 3 APRIL 1976

ALL CLUBS:

WATFORD, AC MILAN, WATFORD, AFC BOURNEMOUTH,
WATFORD, WEST BROMWICH ALBION, BURY, MANSFIELD TOWN

HORNETS APPEARANCES:

APPEARANCES	LEAGUE	FA CUP	LEAGUE CUP	OTHERS
503	415	34	44	10

HORNETS GOALS:

GOALS	LEAGUE	FA CUP	LEAGUE CUP	OTHERS
186	148	15	17	6

STAT ATTACK
LUTHER BLISSETT

ENGLAND INTERNATIONAL:

APPEARANCES	GOALS
14	3

INTERNATIONAL DEBUT:

15 DECEMBER 1982 · ENGLAND 9-0 LUXEMBOURG
(HE SCORED THREE ON HIS DEBUT!)

A major player in the Hornets' rise from lower league obscurity to the First Division, Luther Blissett is a true Watford legend. After turning professional in the 1975/76 season, Blissett went on to become both the club's leading appearance maker and record goalscorer. During the Hornets' debut season in the top flight in 1982/83, he ended the campaign with 27 goals as the country's leading scoring.

Such was Blissett's First Division goalscoring form that international recognition with England soon followed. He marked his full England debut with a hat-trick in England's 9-0 demolition of Luxembourg in a European Championship qualifier.

In total Blissett had three playing spells at Vicarage Road, sandwiched in between stints with AC Milan and Bournemouth. He later enjoyed a successful coaching role at the club under Graham Taylor.

DANGER MEN

ARSENAL
Pierre-Emerick Aubameyang

Pierre-Emerick Aubameyang joined Arsenal in January 2018 for a club record fee, believed to have been in the region of £56M.

The striker was signed from German side Borussia Dortmund and marked his Gunners' debut with a goal. His movement, touch and clinical finishing soon saw him win the hearts of Arsenal fans. Getting the ball to Aubameyang as often as possible is sure to be the aim of new Arsenal boss Unai Emery.

BOURNEMOUTH
Callum Wilson

On his day former Coventry City front man Callum Wilson can be almost unplayable.

Wilson possesses great pace and intelligent off the ball movement that creates space, which in-turn provides chances for him and his teammates. He notched an impressive eight goals in 28 Premier League games last season and began 2018/19 in goalscoring form.

BRIGHTON
Glenn Murray

Now in his second spell with the Seagulls, powerful striker Glenn Murray scored a dozen goals for Brighton last season as the club enjoyed a successful return to the top flight.

His all-round game and goals were the catalyst for Brighton's survival in the Premier League and he will undoubtedly be vital to Chris Hughton's side once again in the new season.

BURNLEY
Matej Vydra

Czech striker Matej Vydra joined Burnley in August 2018 following an outstanding season in the Championship with Derby County.

With a natural eye for goal, Vydra scored 22 goals for the Rams, 21 in the league and ended the 2017/18 term as the Championship's leading marksman. The Clarets will be looking for him to produce the goals at Premier League level.

CARDIFF CITY

Josh Murphy

Flying winger Josh Murphy joined the newly-promoted Bluebirds in the summer of 2018 following Cardiff's elevation to the Premier League.

Recruited from Norwich City, Murphy progressed through the ranks at Carrow Road alongside his twin brother Jacob, who now plays for Newcastle. With electric pace and a real eye for goal, Murphy looks well equipped to impress at the Cardiff City Stadium.

EVERTON

Richarlison

Brazilian winger Richarlison arrived at Goodison Park ahead of the new 2018/19 Premier League season, following a big money move from Watford.

A great deal will be expected of the tricky winger by both his manager and the Everton faithful. Richarlison certainly put down a marker in the opening game of the season when he scored both goals in Everton's 2-2 draw away to Wolverhampton Wanderers.

CHELSEA

Eden Hazard

After starring at the 2018 World Cup with Belgium, Chelsea winger Eden Hazard is sure to be new Blues' boss Maurizio Sarri's go-to man in 2018/19.

With breathtaking close control and exceptional dribbling skills, Hazard is one of the very best talents in the Premier League. The 27-year-old Belgian will undoubtedly be the key to a successful season at Stamford Bridge.

FULHAM

Ryan Sessegnon

Pacy winger Ryan Sessegnon started his career as a left-back before being pushed further forward by Fulham last season.

He scored 16 goals in 52 appearances in 2017/18 as the Cottagers secured promotion to the Premier League after a four-year absence. At just 18 years of age he was voted the 2018 Championship Player of the Season.

CRYSTAL PALACE

Wilfried Zaha

The star of the show for many seasons at Selhurst Park, forward Wilfried Zaha has the pace to worry any defence.

With the ability to simply glide past defenders and into dangerous areas, Zaha is a player who can create chances for teammates as well as contribute with his fair share of goals. The undisputed jewel in the crown at Crystal Palace, his performances are sure to have a major impact on the Eagles' fortunes once again in 2018/19.

HUDDERSFIELD TOWN

Alex Pritchard

The Terriers signed skilful midfield playmaker Alex Pritchard from Norwich City during the January 2018 transfer window.

After helping Huddersfield maintain their top-flight status, Pritchard will now look to shine on the Premier League stage. With neat close control and a wonderful range of passing skills, he's sure to be one of the first names on David Wagner's teamsheet.

DANGER MEN

LEICESTER CITY
James Maddison

James Maddison joined Leicester City on a five-year-deal in the summer of 2018, making a £20M move from Championship club Norwich City.

The attack-minded midfielder, a dead-ball specialist, enjoyed an excellent season with the Canaries in 2017/18. He netted 15 goals in all competitions, including a match-winning strike in the local derby with Ipswich. His form at Carrow Road saw him called up to the England under-21s.

LIVERPOOL
Mohamed Salah

Mohamed Salah produced an outstanding debut campaign at Anfield, and netted an incredible 44 goals in all competitions as Liverpool reached the Champions League Final and finished fourth in the Premier League.

A quick, mobile, hard-working player with great close control, Salah is sure to hold the key to any success Liverpool may enjoy in 2019.

MANCHESTER CITY
Kevin De Bruyne

Midfield genius Kevin De Bruyne was one of many star performers at the Etihad Stadium as Manchester City amassed 100 points and the Premier League title in 2017/18.

De Bruyne has a wide range of passing skills and is one of the very best strikers of a ball from long-range. If the Belgian international is at his best, then Manchester City stand a great chance of retaining their Premier League title.

MANCHESTER UNITED
Romelu Lukaku

Robust striker Romelu Lukaku fired home 16 Premier League goals for Manchester United last season following his big money move from Everton in July 2017.

A left-footed player, Lukaku often uses his immense strength to get the better of defenders and he will certainly be the main focus of the Red Devils' forward play again in 2018/19.

NEWCASTLE UNITED

Salomon Rondon

Venezuelan forward Salomon Rondon moved to St James' Park in August 2018 on a season-long loan deal from West Bromwich Albion, with Dwight Gale heading in the opposite direction.

Rondon netted 24 Premier League goals across three seasons for the Baggies and his strength, hold-up play and aerial prowess made him one of the division's most feared strikers.

SOUTHAMPTON

Nathan Redmond

Attacking England midfielder Nathan Redmond continues to use his pace to break forward and create attacking opportunities for Southampton.

The former Birmingham and Norwich man joined the Saints in June 2016 and scored seven Premier League goals in his first season at St Mary's. A potential match winner, Redmond will be looking to impress new boss Mark Hughes in his first full season in charge of the Saints.

WEST HAM UNITED

Marko Arnautovic

Exciting Austrian forward Marko Arnautovic netted eleven Premier League goals for the Hammers last season.

In what was his debut season with the club, Arnautovic's all-action displays and his direct approach won him many admirers at the London Stadium. He was voted Hammer of the Year last season and is certainly going to be one to watch again in 2018/19.

TOTTENHAM HOTSPUR

Harry Kane

After his goals for England in the 2018 World Cup finals saw him return from Russia with the Golden Boot as the tournament's leading goalscorer, all eyes will once again be on England captain Harry Kane in 2018/19.

An intelligent striker with an incredible goals-to-games ratio - his goals are sure to light up Spurs' new stadium this season.

WOLVERHAMPTON WANDERERS

Ruben Neves

Portuguese midfielder Ruben Neves joined Wolves from Porto last summer for what was then a Championship record fee of around £16M.

The 21-year-old has an excellent range of passing skills and a calm temperament in possession. He loves to strike for goal from distance and looks all set to make a real impression on the Premier League.

Magic MOMENT

13'

WE'RE GOING TO *Wembley*

FIXTURE:	FA Cup semi-final
DATE:	Saturday 14 April 1984
SCORE:	Watford 1 Plymouth Argyle 0
VENUE:	Villa Park
ATTENDANCE:	43,858

Striker George Reilly was the Hornets' hero of the hour as Watford reached the FA Cup final for the first, and only, time in the club's history.

On a sun-drenched afternoon at Villa Park, Plymouth Argyle were the opposition that stood between Watford and a place in the showpiece final.

John Barnes picked up the ball on the half way line and ran almost half the length of the pitch before crossing to George Reilly. The powerful front-man met the ball perfectly and his well-placed near-post header after 13 minutes proved to be the only goal of the game.

Reilly's memorable goal ensured a first trip to Wembley for the club, to face Everton in the final.

CRUDGING

REILLY

BARNES 10

BARNES 10

BARNES 10

REILLY 9

ÉTIENNE CAPOUE

FANTASTIC

WATFORD

There are five England World Cup stars hiding in the crowd... can you find them all?

ANSWERS ON PAGE 62

THE PUSKAS MOVE

Ferenc Puskas is one of the greatest footballers of all time and the creator of the famous 'V' move that you can see used in most games of football. It allows you to change direction quickly and fool your defender. The move is very simple but hard to master at speed.

TIP:
Use this move when you need to lose your defender. Pretend to strike the ball, your opponent will move to block your faked shot, allowing you to move freely in another direction.

TIP:
Always wait until your defender lunges for the ball before performing the Puskas move.

1. Start by dribbling the ball, keep it as near to your foot as possible while moving forward.

2. Move as if to kick the ball, but rather than striking it, bring your foot over the top of the ball.

TIP:
Don't perform this move too often or your opponents will learn to expect it!

3. Use the bottom of your foot to quickly drag the ball back to you.

4. Now change direction. You can finish the move with a shot at goal or by passing to a teammate.

WATFORD

37

ROBERTO
PEREYRA

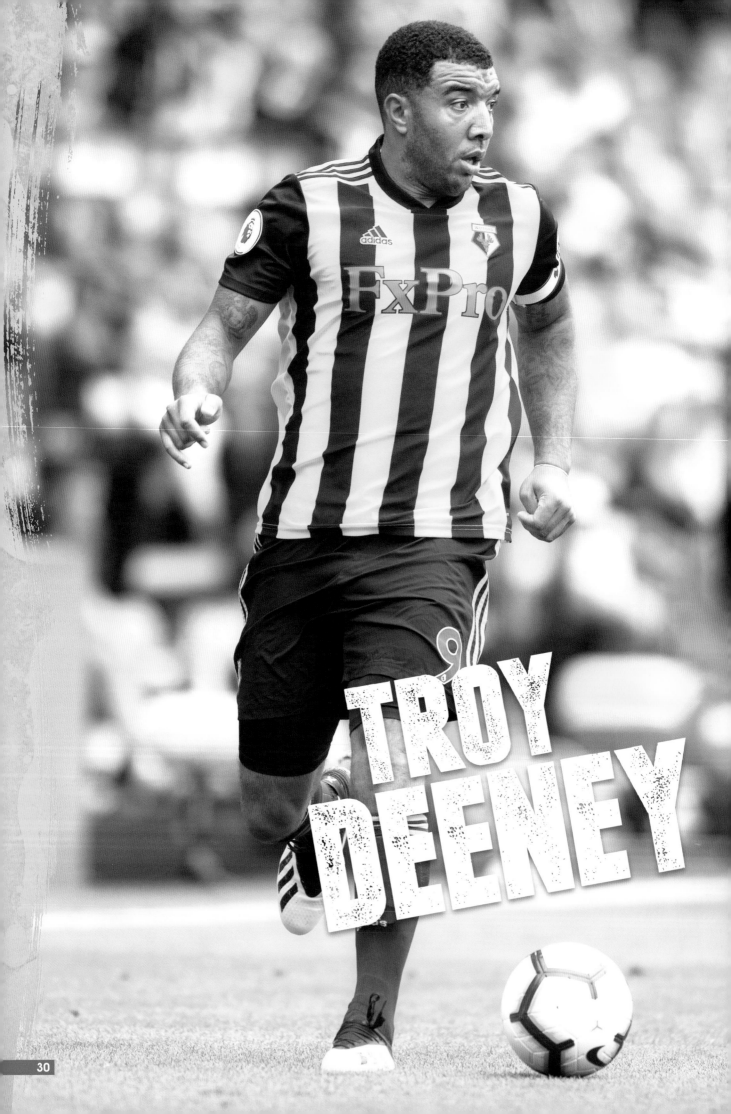

TROY DEENEY

BORN:
11 NOVEMBER 1963 · KINGSTON, JAMAICA

POSITION:
WINGER

HORNETS DEBUT:
WATFORD 1-1 OLDHAM ATHLETIC
SECOND DIVISION · 5 SEPTEMBER 1981

ALL CLUBS:
WATFORD, LIVERPOOL, NEWCASTLE UNITED, CHARLTON ATHLETIC

HORNETS APPEARANCES:

APPEARANCES	LEAGUE	FA CUP	LEAGUE CUP	OTHERS
296	233	31	21	11

HORNETS GOALS:

GOALS	LEAGUE	FA CUP	LEAGUE CUP	OTHERS
85	65	11	7	2

STAT ATTACK
JOHN BARNES

ENGLAND INTERNATIONAL:

APPEARANCES	GOALS
79	11

  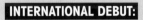

INTERNATIONAL DEBUT:
28 MAY 1983 · ENGLAND 0-0 NORTHERN IRELAND

A top performer for the Hornets in the golden era under Graham Taylor, winger John Barnes made a lasting impression during his time at Vicarage Road.

Barnes played in 36 Second Division fixtures and scored 13 goals as Watford celebrated a historic promotion to the First Division for the first time in the club's history in 1981/82. He then became one of many Watford players who took the First Division by storm in 1982/83 as the Hornets remarkably secured the runners-up spot.

Barnes was also a key performer in the Hornets side that side reached the 1984 FA Cup final. After 296 appearances and 85 goals he joined Liverpool for a fee of £900,000.

ABDOULAYE DOUCOURÉ

There was little debate when it came to the winner of Watford's 2017/18 Graham Taylor OBE Player of the Season award - in fact, he was so impressive that Abdoulaye Doucouré also took home the Players' Player of the Season trophy at the end of his best campaign so far.

In a season when the Hornets' goals were spread throughout the entire squad - with no fewer than 17 different players finding the net - Doucouré topped the charts from midfield with seven, six of which came in a stunning run of form between the start of the season and Christmas

In fact he opened his tally on the first day, scoring in a thrilling 3-3 draw with Liverpool before contributing to a 2-0 win at Southampton, and then starting the comeback from two goals down to draw 2-2 at West Brom.

Goals in defeats to Chelsea and Manchester United followed, as did an outstanding curling effort from distance - probably his best strike yet - in a home game against Huddersfield. A last-minute equaliser against Southampton in January 2018 was to be his last of the season, but it was more than just goals which contributed to the Frenchman's landslide victory in the Player of the Season running.

His 39 appearances in all competitions made him a near ever-present in the Hornets' side, and the stats show no other Watford player made more touches, passes and tackles in Premier League action that term. That's not to mention his three assists - bettered only by José Holebas and Richarlison, who made four each.

Despite attracting serious attention from some of England's biggest clubs, Doucouré committed his long-term future to Watford by signing a new five-year contract before the start of the current campaign, and promptly excited supporters by claiming 'the best is yet to come' in an interview with the club's matchday programme. What a prospect!

PLAYER OF THE SEASON

GOAL
OF THE SEASON

DARYL JANMAAT V CHELSEA (H)
MONDAY FEBRUARY 5, 2018

On a night that will live long in the memory of every Watford fan who was there, Daryl Janmaat scored an equally unforgettable goal as the Hornets saw off reigning Premier League champions Chelsea in an incredible 4-1 win.

It was Javi Gracia's first home game as Watford's Head Coach and his Vicarage Road reign could not have started any better. The Hornets had won only one of their previous 12 Premier League matches, so to gain three points here was not only a surprise, it was extremely important.

Gracia's side were already on top when Chelsea midfielder Tiémoué Bakayoko was sent off for a second bookable offence with half-an-hour played, and when Gerard Deulofeu was fouled by goalkeeper Thibaut Courtois in the box, Troy Deeney converted the penalty to make it 1-0 moments before the break.

Watford appeared to be hanging on until an excellent Eden Hazard curler levelled the scores with just eight minutes to go, but the Golden Boys had another gear and were to score three more in the game's closing stages - the pick of the bunch undoubtedly the fine solo effort which went on to earn Janmaat the club's 2017/18 Goal of the Season trophy.

Just two minutes had passed since Hazard's equaliser when the Dutchman cut inside from the right-flank and played a clever one-two with Roberto Pereyra, eliminating a handful of defenders in the process, before firing back across Courtois and into the far corner with his weaker left foot. It was a goal of some quality, and more than worthy of restoring Watford's lead against Antonio Conte's men.

Deulofeu and Pereyra added a goal each to round off one of those nights under the Vicarage Road floodlights, but it is Janmaat's strike which will forever be associated with this uplifting victory.

GUESS THE CLUB

Can you work out which European Club each set of clues is pointing to?

1 ANSWER

3 ANSWER

2 ANSWER

4 ANSWER

5 ANSWER

8 ANSWER

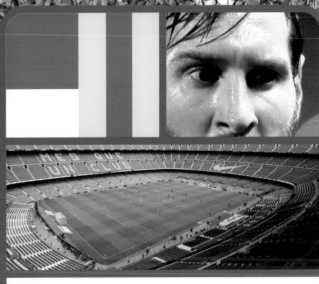

6 ANSWER

9 ANSWER

7 ANSWER

10 ANSWER

ANSWERS ON PAGE 62

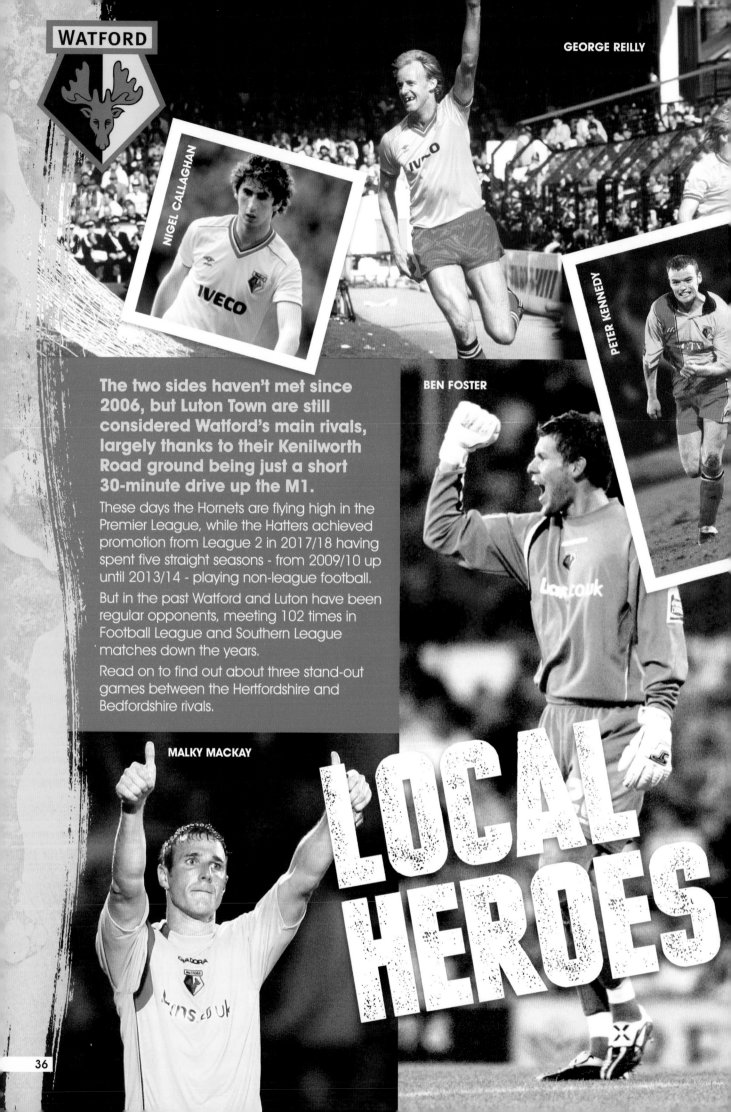

GEORGE REILLY

NIGEL CALLAGHAN

PETER KENNEDY

BEN FOSTER

The two sides haven't met since 2006, but Luton Town are still considered Watford's main rivals, largely thanks to their Kenilworth Road ground being just a short 30-minute drive up the M1.

These days the Hornets are flying high in the Premier League, while the Hatters achieved promotion from League 2 in 2017/18 having spent five straight seasons - from 2009/10 up until 2013/14 - playing non-league football.

But in the past Watford and Luton have been regular opponents, meeting 102 times in Football League and Southern League matches down the years.

Read on to find out about three stand-out games between the Hertfordshire and Bedfordshire rivals.

MALKY MACKAY

LOCAL HEROES

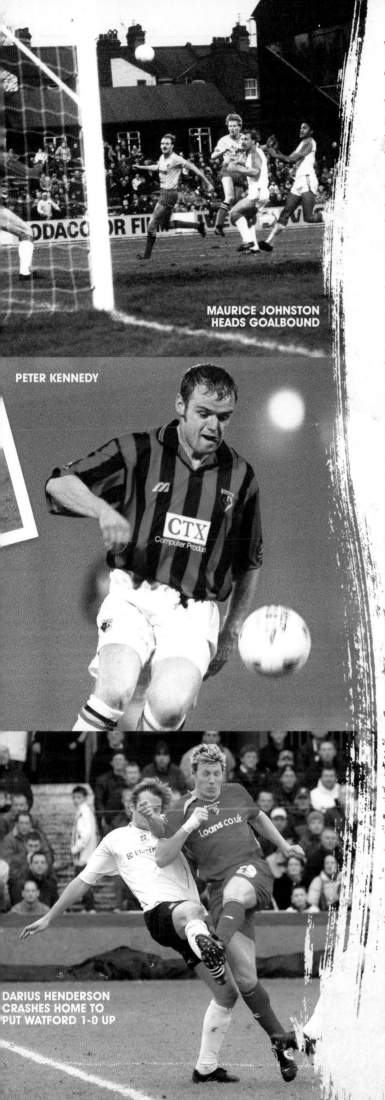

MAURICE JOHNSTON HEADS GOALBOUND

PETER KENNEDY

DARIUS HENDERSON CRASHES HOME TO PUT WATFORD 1-0 UP

WATFORD 4-3 LUTON TOWN
TUESDAY JANUARY 10, 1984

Watford's 1983/84 FA Cup campaign famously resulted in the club's first ever major final, but did you know the Hornets' road to Wembley started with an enthralling replay win over Luton Town?

Having drawn the initial third round tie 2-2 at Kenilworth Road – with John Barnes and Mo Johnston forcing a replay after the hosts had taken a two-goal lead - Watford needed extra-time to eventually see off the Hatters three days later in a memorable 4-3 win.

Barnes, Nigel Callaghan and George Reilly all scored in normal time under the Vicarage Road floodlights, before Johnston netted for the fourth game running to set up a fourth round tie with Charlton.

Brighton, Birmingham and Plymouth were dispatched in later rounds, and the Graham Taylor-inspired cup run eventually ended with defeat to Everton under the famous twin towers of Wembley.

LUTON TOWN 0-4 WATFORD
SATURDAY OCTOBER 4, 1997

Probably the Hornets' most famous win over their rivals Luton, Watford saw off the Hatters with a relentless first half display which saw them four goals to the good with only half-an-hour played.

Richard Johnson got the ball rolling just five minutes in, a lead which was doubled by Dai Thomas as the travelling contingent packed into the away end started to realise they were witnessing an afternoon of football they'd never forget.

Two Peter Kennedy goals in as many minutes made the advantage four, and it was perhaps inevitable that - having raced into such a commanding position - Watford took their foot off the gas after the break and cruised to a comfortable victory.

Ten years had passed since their last league victory over Luton - a 2-0 home win in April 1987 - but this was well and truly worth the wait.

LUTON TOWN 1-2 WATFORD
MONDAY JANUARY 2, 2006

Watford's most recent win against the Hatters was a significant one, coming midway through a surprise push for promotion under then-manager Aidy Boothroyd.

Meeting at Kenilworth Road just after the turn of the year, Darius Henderson put the Hornets ahead nine minutes in and the lead was extended by Malky Mackay on the half-hour, despite claims from the hosts that the defender's header hadn't crossed the line.

Carlos Edwards gave Luton some hope by scoring early in the second half, but Watford clung on to the three points - despite Ashley Young's sending off - thanks in no small part to some impressive goalkeeping from Ben Foster.

The Golden Boys went on to finish the 2005/06 campaign in third and secured an unlikely return to Premier League football thanks to a play-off final victory over Leeds in Cardiff.

Magic MOMENT

24'

GOING *Up!*

FIXTURE: Championship Play-Off final

DATE: Sunday 21 May 2006

SCORE: Watford 3 Leeds United 0

VENUE: Millennium Stadium

ATTENDANCE: 64,736

YOUNG **15**   SULLIVAN **1**

DeMERIT **6**

6 DeMERIT

American defender Jay DeMerit capped off a memorable 2005/06 season with the Hornets as he headed home the first goal of the Play-Off final victory over Leeds United at the Millennium Stadium.

DeMerit met an Ashley Young corner with a bullet-like header after 25 minutes. His goal set Aidy Boothroyd's team up for a comfortable 3-0 victory and promotion to the Premier League

The goal was a fitting reward for DeMerit, who played 37 games in the 2005/06 season while forming an impressive central-defensive partnership with Malky Mackay.

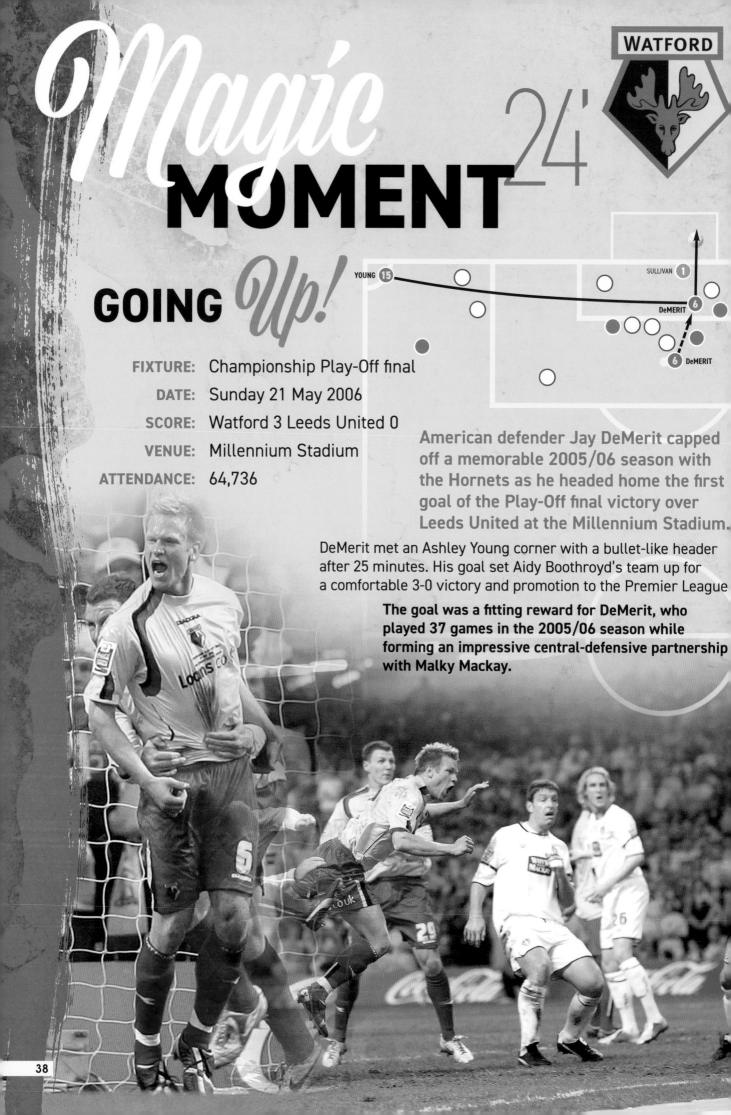

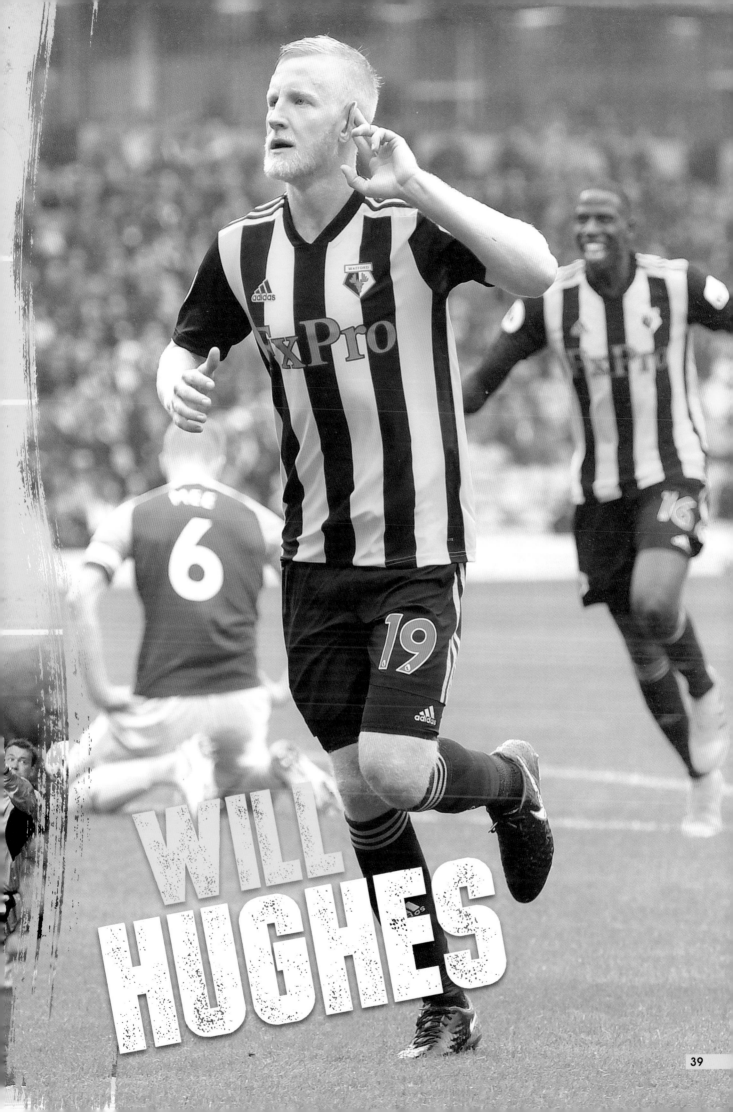

WILL
HUGHES

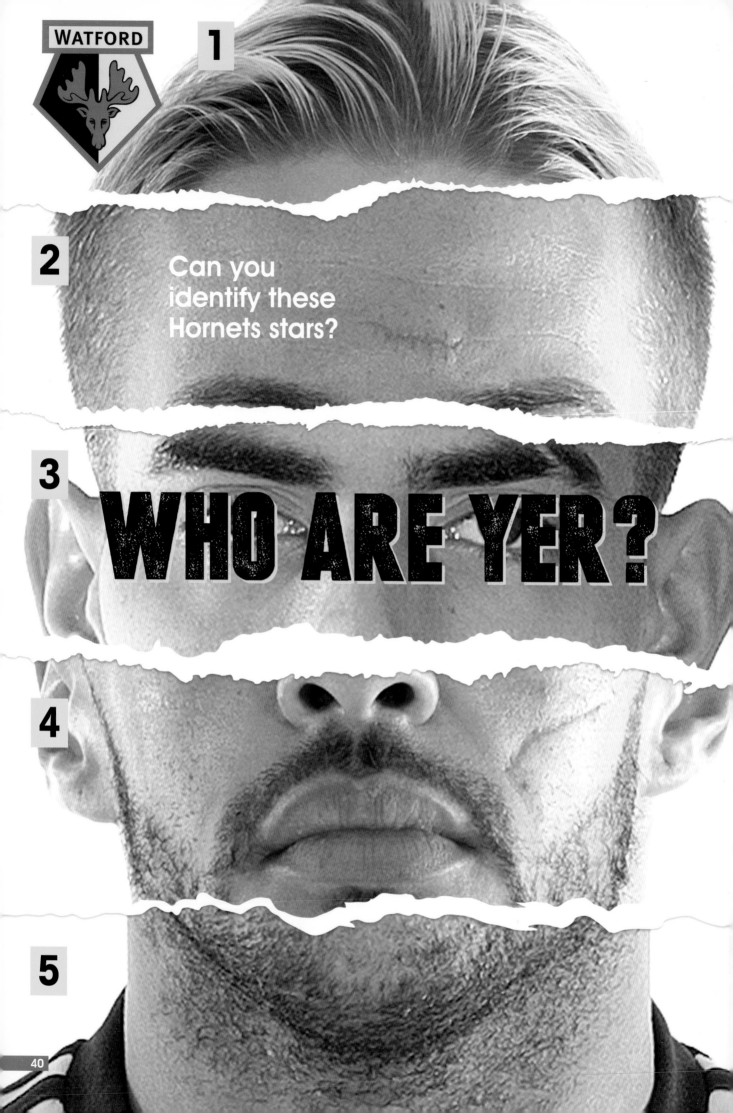

WATFORD

1

2

Can you
identify these
Hornets stars?

3

WHO ARE YER?

4

5

6

7

8

10

9

ANSWERS ON PAGE 62

WATFORD

ISAAC SUCCESS

#BOY'SGOTSKILLS
THE FLIP FLAP

Practise! Practise! Practise!

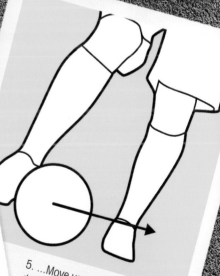

1. Start by getting familiar with the leg movement.

Push the ball with the outside of your foot.

TIP: Try performing the movement while hopping

TIP: Practise performing the movement while moving forwards and backwards

2. Then move your foot around the ball and bring it back in towards your body.

AKA 'the Elastico'

This move is used by many players and was made famous first by Rivelino in the 1970s and more recently by Ronaldinho. It is a simple technique and done right, really works! The idea behind it is to unbalance your defender by moving the ball one way before using some tricky footwork to move off in another direction!

3. Once you're familiar with the movement, try it while dribbling the ball forward.

TIP: Work on perfecting the technique, then when you're ready you can start moving the ball further away from your body to really confuse your defender

4. Push the ball with the outside of your foot, away from your body. As your defender moves in the direction of the ball...

5. ...Move your foot around the ball, drag it back across your body and move off in the other direction.

43

We take a look at three great Hornets games from last season...

◀◀ REWIND

WATFORD 2-1 ARSENAL
SATURDAY OCTOBER 14, 2017

After late, late shows against Swansea and West Brom, it couldn't happen for a third consecutive game, could it?

When Troy Deeney's 71st-minute penalty cancelled out a first-half Per Mertesacker opener, the Hornets were galvanised and piled towards the Gunners' goal, believing three points were within their reach.

Nearly 90 seconds of stoppage time had passed when a blocked Étienne Capoue effort fell kindly for Tom Cleverley, who thrillingly lashed home the loose ball in front of a jubilant Rookery Stand as Watford earned a first home win over Arsenal in nearly 30 years.

WATFORD 4-1 CHELSEA
MONDAY FEBRUARY 5, 2018

It was Javi Gracia's first game in the Vicarage Road dugout and there was a special atmosphere under the floodlights as the Premier League champions came to town.

Watford took a deserved lead late in the first half when Troy Deeney slammed home a penalty against a Chelsea side down to 10 men after Tiémoué Bakayoko's dismissal.

Eden Hazard's 82nd-minute equaliser felt harsh on the Hornets, but up stepped Daryl Janmaat just moments after the restart, gliding past two defenders before eliminating three more thanks to a clever one-two with Roberto Pereyra and poking into the bottom corner to restore the advantage in some style.

It was a strike worthy of winning the club's Goal of the Season award, and it was soon followed by Gerard Deulofeu and Pereyra efforts as Watford coasted to a stunning 4-1 win.

WATFORD 1-0 WEST BROM
SATURDAY MARCH 3, 2018

The Hornets had defeated Everton by a single goal a week previous, and they saw off West Brom by the same margin when returning to The Vic seven days later.

A small army of fans had arrived early to help clear the snow, and they were treated to a third successive home win as Watford crucially increased the gap between themselves and the bottom three to nine points.

In a game of few chances, the Hornets needed to be clinical, and they were just that as Troy Deeney bore down on goal after Will Hughes' precision pass and coolly clipped over the on-rushing Ben Foster with 13 minutes remaining.

This was by no means a classic encounter, but it felt like a significant three points as Watford went on to ensure a fourth successive season of Premier League football.

1

Who made the most league appearances last season?

ANSWER

2

Who was the last player to join the Hornets on a permanent deal in the 2017 summer transfer window?

ANSWER

3

Who top scored last season with seven league goals?

ANSWER

4

Last season, Watford's highest goalscoring performance was against which team and what was the score?

ANSWER

5

How many clean sheets did Watford keep in the Premier League in 2017/18?

ANSWER

6

Who put in the most tackles, with 79, last season?

ANSWER

2017/18 END OF TERM EXAM

How much did you learn about the Hornets' last campaign?

7

Who was Watford's first win of the 2017/18 season against?

ANSWER

8

Which Hornets player received the most yellow cards in the Premier League last season?

ANSWER

9

Which team did Watford knock out of the FA Cup in the third round?

ANSWER

10

How many goals did the Hornets score in the Premier League last season?

ANSWER

ANSWERS ON PAGE 62

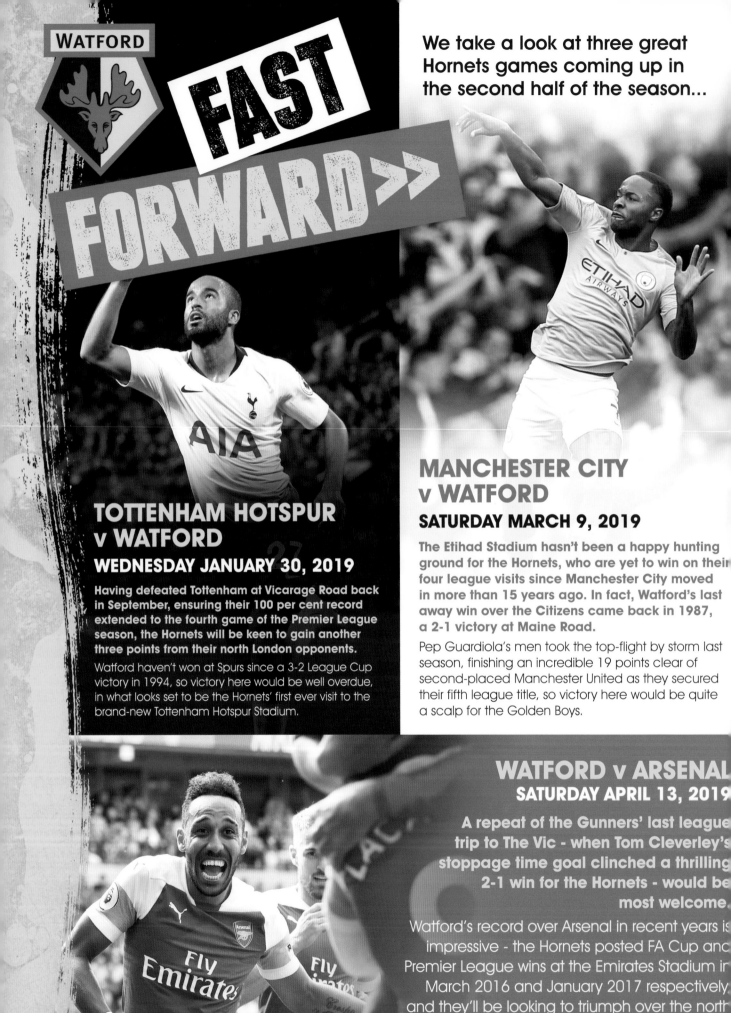

FAST FORWARD >>

We take a look at three great Hornets games coming up in the second half of the season...

TOTTENHAM HOTSPUR v WATFORD
WEDNESDAY JANUARY 30, 2019

Having defeated Tottenham at Vicarage Road back in September, ensuring their 100 per cent record extended to the fourth game of the Premier League season, the Hornets will be keen to gain another three points from their north London opponents.

Watford haven't won at Spurs since a 3-2 League Cup victory in 1994, so victory here would be well overdue, in what looks set to be the Hornets' first ever visit to the brand-new Tottenham Hotspur Stadium.

MANCHESTER CITY v WATFORD
SATURDAY MARCH 9, 2019

The Etihad Stadium hasn't been a happy hunting ground for the Hornets, who are yet to win on their four league visits since Manchester City moved in more than 15 years ago. In fact, Watford's last away win over the Citizens came back in 1987, a 2-1 victory at Maine Road.

Pep Guardiola's men took the top-flight by storm last season, finishing an incredible 19 points clear of second-placed Manchester United as they secured their fifth league title, so victory here would be quite a scalp for the Golden Boys.

WATFORD v ARSENAL
SATURDAY APRIL 13, 2019

A repeat of the Gunners' last league trip to The Vic - when Tom Cleverley's stoppage time goal clinched a thrilling 2-1 win for the Hornets - would be most welcome.

Watford's record over Arsenal in recent years is impressive - the Hornets posted FA Cup and Premier League wins at the Emirates Stadium in March 2016 and January 2017 respectively, and they'll be looking to triumph over the north Londoners once more as the season draws closer to its conclusion

PREDICTION FOR
PREMIER LEAGUE WINNERS:

Liverpool

YOUR
PREDICTION:

PREDICTION FOR
CHAMPIONSHIP WINNERS:

Swansea City

YOUR
PREDICTION:

PREDICTION FOR FA CUP WINNERS:

Watford

YOUR
PREDICTION:

PREDICTION FOR
PREMIER LEAGUE RUNNERS-UP:

Man City

YOUR
PREDICTION:

PREDICTION FOR
CHAMPIONSHIP RUNNERS-UP:

Derby County

YOUR
PREDICTION:

2018/19 PREDICTIONS

Here are our
predictions for
the 2018/19 season.

**What do you think
will happen?**

PREDICTION FOR PREMIER LEAGUE
TOP SCORER:

Harry Kane

YOUR
PREDICTION:

PREDICTION FOR CHAMPIONSHIP
TOP SCORER:

Oli McBurnie

YOUR
PREDICTION:

PREDICTION FOR LEAGUE
CUP WINNERS:

Burnley

YOUR
PREDICTION:

#BOY'S GOT SKILLS
THE OKOCHA STEP OVER

Jay-Jay Okocha was one of the best tricksters the Premier League has ever seen. He was effortless in getting past his opponents and here we take a look at how to perform one of his most famous moves...

1. While running...

...roll the ball with the inside of your right foot across your body to the left.

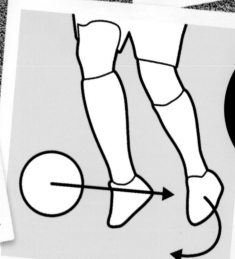

2. Fake like you're going to hit it with your left foot...

TIP: Roll the ball far enough out across your body so it doesn't get stuck under your feet.

Tip: Practise until you can master the move off both feet!

3. ...but step over it instead!

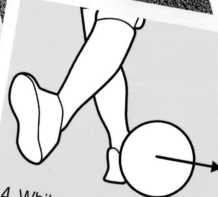

4. While you're performing the step over...

...do a quick body feint to the right to help throw off your opponent.

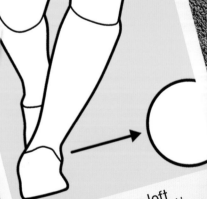

5. Continue going left...

...leaving you opponent wonderin what just happened

48

WATFORD

BEN FOSTER

GREAT GAFFERS

Watford have been blessed with a host of great managers over the years - here we take a brief look at four of our finest.

GRAHAM TAYLOR

The arrival of Graham Taylor at Vicarage Road in June 1977 saw the club embark on an incredible adventure as he guided the Hornets from the Fourth to First Division.

During this golden era at Vicarage Road, Taylor nurtured talents including Luther Blissett, John Barnes, Nigel Callaghan and Maurice Johnston as the Hornets took the top flight by storm.

He guided the club to the runners-up slot in the First Division during their debut campaign in the top flight, and also to a first Wembley appearance in the 1984 FA Cup Final.

After spells with Aston Villa, England and Wolves, he returned to Watford for a second spell in charge in 1996 and led the team to the Second Division title (third tier) in 1997/98 and Wembley glory twelve months later via the First Division play-offs.

QUIQUE SANCHEZ FLORES

A much travelled and vastly experienced manager, Spaniard Flores was appointed Watford's head coach on 5 June 2016.

He arrived at Vicarage Road as a replacement for Slavisa Jokanovic as the club prepared to compete in the Premier League having secured promotion as Championship runners-up the previous season.

Under his guidance the Hornets achieved their aim of Premier League survival as they comfortably amassed 45 points and secured a 13th placed finish.

An excellent December included a 3-0 demolition of Liverpool at The Vic and saw Flores named Manager of the Month. He also led Watford to the 2016 FA Cup semi-final before leaving the club at the end of the campaign.

GIANFRANCO ZOLA

After a glittering playing career in his native Italy and in England with Chelsea, Zola took his first steps in management with West Ham United, before becoming boss at Vicarage Road in the summer of 2012.

Zola wasted little time in impressing once in control at Watford and guided the club to a third place finish in the Championship in his first season at the helm.

The Hornets missed out on automatic promotion by just two points before engaging in an unforgettable play-off semi-final with Leicester City, which Watford won 3-2 on aggregate following the most dramatic of games during the second leg at Vicarage Road.

Sadly the play-off final just proved to be a bridge too far as Zola's side narrowly lost 1-0 to Crystal Palace after extra-time. With the team unable to shrug off the disappointment of the near-miss the previous season, Zola resigned in December 2013.

AIDY BOOTHROYD

Having gained a growing reputation in the game following impressive youth coaching roles at Peterborough United, Norwich City and West Bromwich Albion, Boothroyd also coached at Leeds United before being named Watford boss in March 2005.

His appointment was seen as something of a gamble by the Hornets' Board, but it certainly proved to be a gamble that soon paid off. In his first full season at Vicarage Road, Boothroyd plotted Watford's 2005/06 promotion from the Championship via the end of season play-offs.

After finishing third in the Championship table, Watford beat Crystal Place at the semi-final stage before seeing off Leeds United in the final at Cardiff's Millennium Stadium.

Boothroyd also guided the club to the FA Cup semi-final in 2007 before leaving the club in 2008.

FIRST ELEVEN

Choose your all-time First Eleven, put their names and numbers on the back of the shirts, then colour them in!

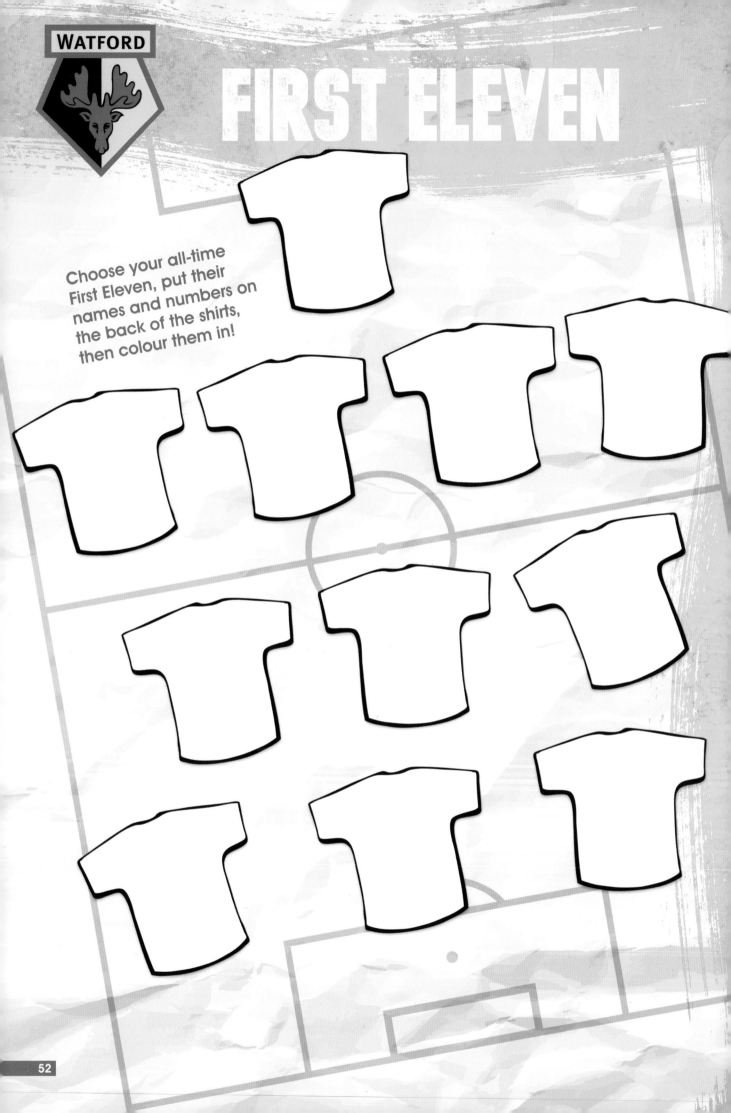

SPOT THE BALL

The ball is missing from this photo, where should it be?

WHAT BALL?

Can you figure out which is the real ball in this photo?

ABDOULAYE DOUCOURÉ

BORN:

9 JULY 1985 · STEVENAGE, HERTFORDSHIRE

POSITION:

WINGER

HORNETS DEBUT:

WATFORD 3-1 MILLWALL
NATIONWIDE DIVISION ONE · 13 SEPTEMBER 2003

ALL CLUBS:

WATFORD, ASTON VILLA, MANCHESTER UNITED

HORNETS APPEARANCES:

APPEARANCES	LEAGUE	FA CUP	LEAGUE CUP
110	101	1	8

HORNETS GOALS:

GOALS	LEAGUE	LEAGUE CUP
22	20	2

STAT ATTACK
ASHLEY YOUNG

ENGLAND INTERNATIONAL:

APPEARANCES	GOALS
39	7

INTERNATIONAL DEBUT:

16 NOVEMBER 2007 · AUSTRIA 0-1 ENGLAND
(STATS CORRECT AS OF 31 JULY 2018)

One of England's heroes from the 2018 World Cup finals in Russia, Ashley Young began his career at Watford and played 110 times for the Hornets scoring 22 goals, before sealing big money moves to Aston Villa and subsequently Manchester United.

Young broke into the Hornets' first team under the management of Ray Lewington in the 2003/04 season and became a regular in 2004/05 campaign. Under the management of Aidy Boothroyd in 2005/06, Young really made his mark and helped Watford win promotion to the Premier League via the play-offs.

Once in the top flight, Young's pace, trickery and eye for goal plus his ability to provide chances for others swiftly alerted a number of other Premier League clubs and Watford eventually accepted a bid of £8M for him from Aston Villa in January 2007.

HERO HUNT

Here is a list of 20 Hornets heroes. All but one of their surnames are hidden in the grid.

Can you work out who is missing?

```
C R M I P I O S G H D E F M W L S B E T P E
D H A G Z V E Y S P H E B I R H W U B E D O
A Q T F A W D R S I A E J C D E M E R I T D
A E A I A Y G T U O N R T F A L A O Q V T E
N A B E M X F I K R V O B Z K G F N P O M B
J K R S E S L E P D T L Y I C U I X Z E U B
A M E W F C L C U H N Y I E M S M H D N D L
C H J S H U R H V Y A A O G F O F N N L U C
K K C N B L I S S E T T L K X N Q T O U U O
E T I G B L N W P D T C J L Q S B A B T I D
T W U B H I H T J W G G P Y E O J Z P S O A
T H B B E O L R L S V R N V S L G R E B O C
O I O X L N G Z V H T B S S B C C E Z A H I
U V E T V M O Y U A F A K V R N L C U A A M
W E O R E X I R Q T K A B I S E T D M X H F
V N N N F C K M T Y C U A P E J K B B N A M
R P D F A E J L H S I S V C I N E G B L G O
T E E I P U Y E N O O M R Q O R M N R I M N
A L S H D T J A P N M R A F L U T E K J I U
E S B S X K O I B H A E P A O Z T X L I U W
S S Q A R S H G V U D K I R H B Q D H O N P
W R V C R W B O Y O U N G Y B O S E L M N S
T Z U F U N A W E T B B X F M G T T N Y T Q
A I D O Y L E Y D Q R G F O E E D Y H I U S
C R J B U P O S Z A M E S I S U K W J H L O
```

I ♥ WFC

John **Barnes**	Jay **DeMerit**	Micah **Hyde**	Wilf **Rostron**
Luther **Blissett**	Lloyd **Doyley**	Kenny **Jackett**	Stewart **Scullion**
Dennis **Bond**	Nigel **Gibbs**	Ross **Jenkins**	Tommy **Smith**
Alec **Chamberlain**	Heidar **Helguson**	John **McClelland**	Les **Taylor**
Tony **Coton**	Cliff **Holton**	Tommy **Mooney**	Ashley **Young**

ANSWERS ON PAGE 62

RLVOELPOI 1

ALUMHF 2

FEEHFLDIS NIEUDT 3

RNGBIHMMIA TIYC 4

TEWS AMH DUTNIE 5

YCTSLRA LAPEAC 6

Here are the away shirts of twelve football clubs, but their team names have been jumbled up!

Can you figure out who's who?

SHIRT**SHUFFLE**

OONEUMTBRUH 7

NQESEU RKAP GRARNES 8

KOETS TCIY 9

WESATNELC TUNEDI 10

ROTPENS HRTNO NDE 11

NATOS LAVIL 12

57

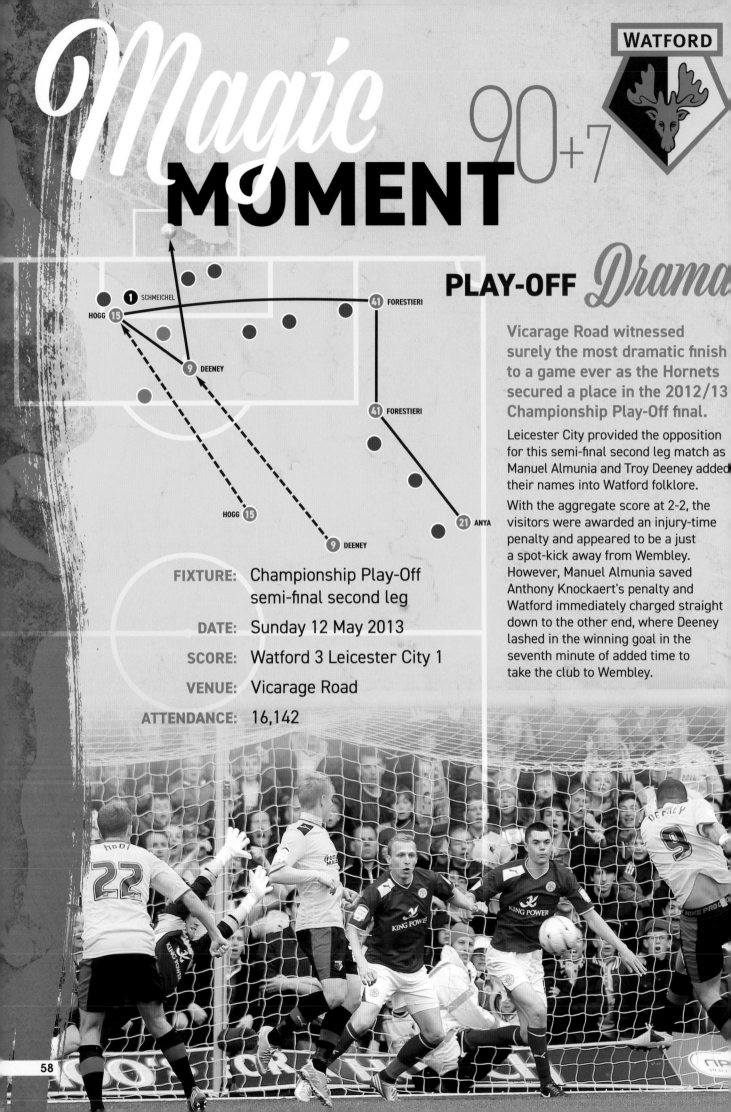

Magic
MOMENT

90+7

WATFORD

PLAY-OFF *Drama*

SCHMEICHEL 1

HOGG 15

9 DEENEY

41 FORESTIERI

41 FORESTIERI

HOGG 15

9 DEENEY

21 ANYA

Vicarage Road witnessed surely the most dramatic finish to a game ever as the Hornets secured a place in the 2012/13 Championship Play-Off final.

Leicester City provided the opposition for this semi-final second leg match as Manuel Almunia and Troy Deeney added their names into Watford folklore.

With the aggregate score at 2-2, the visitors were awarded an injury-time penalty and appeared to be a just a spot-kick away from Wembley. However, Manuel Almunia saved Anthony Knockaert's penalty and Watford immediately charged straight down to the other end, where Deeney lashed in the winning goal in the seventh minute of added time to take the club to Wembley.

FIXTURE:	Championship Play-Off semi-final second leg
DATE:	Sunday 12 May 2013
SCORE:	Watford 3 Leicester City 1
VENUE:	Vicarage Road
ATTENDANCE:	16,142

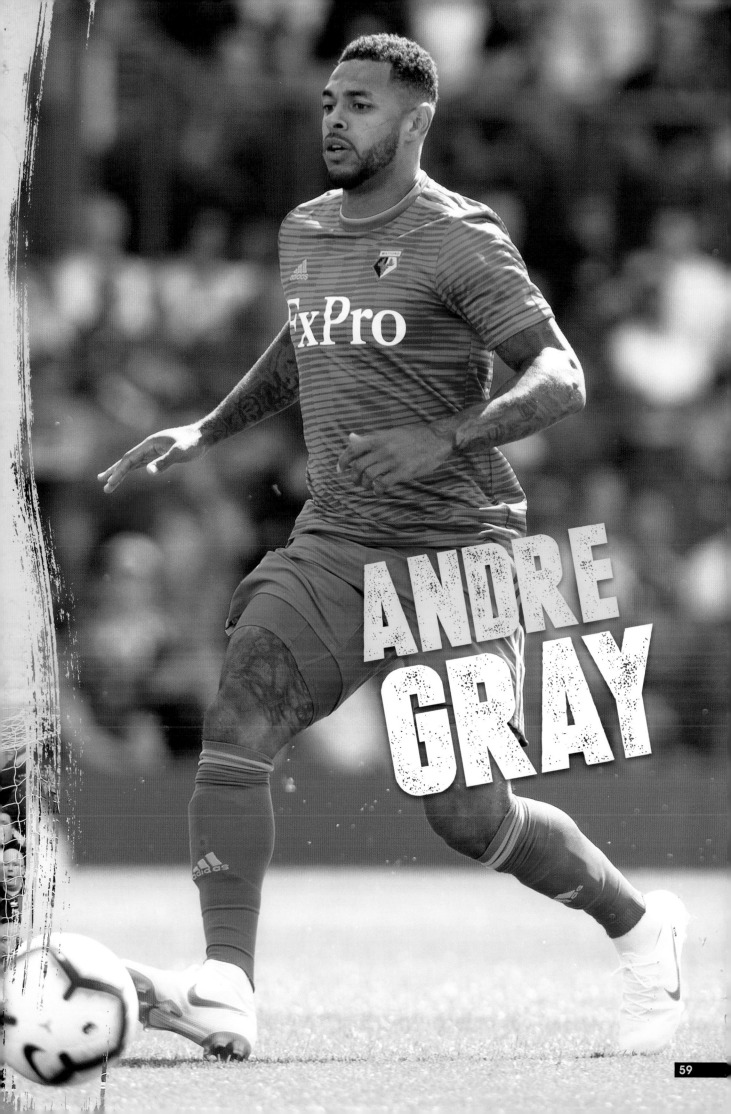

ANDRE
GRAY

How's your knowledge of the laws of the game?
You think you can do better than the man in the middle?
here's your chance to prove it...

HEY REF!

1. Troy Deeney shoots for goal from 25 yards. His fierce drive deflects off your head, wrong-footing the keeper, on its way into the back of the net. What's your call?

A: You award an indirect free-kick to the opposition.
B: It's a goal!
C: You give a drop-ball from where you were hit with ball.

2. Andre Gray strikes for goal from six yards, but as he shoots, the ball bursts and stops just before the goal line. Alert, he follows up and taps the ball home. What's your call?

A: It's a goal!
B: You award a penalty kick to the Hornets.
C: No goal and you restart with a drop ball where the ball burst.

3. Troy Deeney sends the keeper the wrong way from the penalty spot, but his effort hits the post and rebounds straight to Andre Gray who rifles the ball into the net to score. What is your decision?

A: It's a goal!
B: The spot kick has to be retaken.
C: You award an indirect free-kick to the opposition.

DEENEY

DEENEY   GRAY

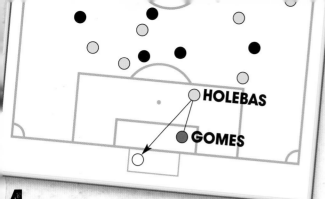

4.

Heurelho Gomes attempts to take a quick goal kick, but to his horror, it hits José Holebas who is still in the penalty area and the ball deflects into his own net. What's your call, ref?

A: It's a goal!

B: A corner kick to the opposing team

C: The goal kick has to be retaken.

5.

Standing in his own penalty area, Heurelho Gomes catches the ball directly from teammate José Holebas' throw-in. What is your decision?

A: Everything's fine. Play on.

B: You award the opposing team an indirect free-kick.

C: A yellow card for Gomes and a penalty for the opposing team.

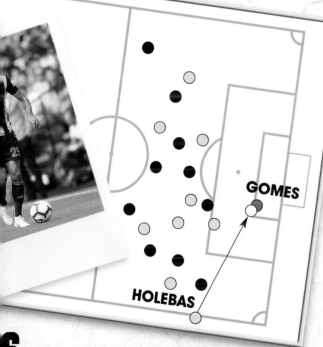

6.

You have decided Andre Gray's spot kick must be re-taken after an infringement by the keeper. This time Troy Deeney steps forward to take the kick. Is that allowed?

A: No, I award an indirect free kick to the opposition.

B: Yes, any Hornets player can re-take the penalty.

C: No, the player who took the initial spot kick, Andre Gray, must retake the kick.

7.

You have awarded a drop ball. As you drop the ball, José Holebas and the opposing player both kick the ball at exactly the same time before it hits the turf. What's your ruling?

A: You show a yellow card to both players for ungentlemanly conduct.

B: You drop the ball again.

C: Play on.

8.

Andre Gray is on the scoresheet again, tapping in from only three yards out. When he scores, he is slightly ahead of the last defender, but in line with the goalkeeper. What is your decision?

A: Goal. In line with the keeper is not offside.

B: Goal disallowed. Gray is offside. To be onside, he must be in line with the second last opponent or the ball.

C: Goal. A player can't be offside inside the six-yard box.

9.

Troy Deeney takes a long throw in aiming for the head of Miguel Britos. No-one makes contact with the ball and it bounces into the net direct from Deeney's throw. What's your call, ref?

A: Goal. Providing there was an attempt to play the ball.

B: Goal. As long as the throw-in was taken correctly.

C: No Goal. A goal can never be scored direct from a throw in.

ANSWERS ON PAGE 62

ANSWERS

PAGE 26 · FANTASTIC

Harry Kane, Jordan Henderson, Raheem Sterling, Jordan Pickford and Harry Maguire.

PAGE 53 · SPOT THE BALL

PAGE 34 · GUESS THE CLUB

1. Ajax. 2. Paris Saint-Germain.
3. Bayern Munich. 4. Sporting Lisbon.
5. Real Madrid. 6. Arsenal. 7. Celtic.
8. Juventus. 9. Barcelona. 10. Club Brugge

PAGE 53 · WHAT BALL?

Ball F

PAGE 56 · HERO HUNT

Nigel Gibbs

PAGE 40 · WHO ARE YER?

1. Sebastian Prödl. 2. Tom Cleverley.
3. Adam Masina. 4. Andre Gray.
5. Troy Deeney. 6. José Holebas.
7. Isaac Success. 8. Will Hughes.
9. Daryl Janmaat. 10. Kiko Femenía.

PAGE 57 · SHIRT SHUFFLE

1. Liverpool. 2. Fulham.
3. Sheffield United. 4. Birmingham City.
5. West Ham United. 6. Crystal Palace.
7. Bournemouth. 8. Queens Park Rangers.
9. Stoke City. 10. Newcastle United.
11. Preston North End. 12. Aston Villa.

PAGE 45
2017/18 END OF TERM EXAM

1. Richarlison, 38 appearances. 2. Marvin Zeegelaar. 3. Abdoulaye Doucoure.
4. Watford 4 Chelsea 1. 5. 9. 6. Abdoulaye Doucouré. 7. AFC Bournemouth.
8. Abdoulaye Doucouré, 10 yellow cards.
9. Bristol City. 10. 44.

PAGE 60 · HEY REF!

1. B. 2. C. 3. A. 4. C. 5. B.
6. B. 7. B. 8. B. 9. C.